*B*lankenship BASIC

John Blankenship

Produced by:
Brian Wiser & Bill Martens

 Apple PugetSound Program Library Exchange

Blankenship BASIC

Copyright © 2018 by Apple Pugetsound Program Library Exchange (A.P.P.L.E.)
All Rights Reserved.

www.callapple.org

ISBN: 978-1-387-91791-4

ACKNOWLEDGEMENTS

Blankenship BASIC was programmed by John Blankenship and Cecil Fretwell of A.P.P.L.E., and that software is copyright © 1984-1987, 2018 by John Blankenship.

This new book, produced in coordination with John Blankenship, is copyright by A.P.P.L.E.. No claim to copyright over *Blankenship BASIC* is created outside of those portions created by A.P.P.L.E..

Thanks to John Blankenship for the original manual, Robert Knepp for the ProDOS version of the software, and Bill Martens for the DOS 3.3 version of the software.

The Cover and Book were designed by Brian Wiser.

PRODUCTION

Brian Wiser → Design, Layout, Editing
Bill Martens → Scanning, Retyping

DISCLAIMER

About the Author

John Blankenship

John Blankenship taught programming, robotics, and engineering technology at DeVry University for 33 years. He holds a Masters Degree in Electronic Engineering Technology from Southern Polytechnic State University, an MBA from Georgia State University, and a BSEE from Virginia Polytechnic State University.

During his early teaching years, John created *Blankenship BASIC* for the Apple II computer and other programs like *Speech Development System*. He wrote magazine articles for publications such as *Byte*, and numerous Apple books including *Apple House*, *Robotic Arm Projects*, and *Structured BASIC Programming in BBASIC*.

After retiring from DeVry, he wanted to develop better methods for teaching and motivating precollege students. John, along with colleague Samuel Mishal, developed *RobotBASIC* for Windows – a programming language ideally suited to the educational environment. And, because of their desire to contribute to the Science, Technology, Engineering and Mathematics (STEM) movement, John and Sam continue to make *RobotBASIC* available to schools, teachers, and students absolutely free from RobotBASIC.org.

About the Producers

Brian Wiser

Brian Wiser is a producer of books, films, games, and events, as well as a long-time consultant, enthusiast and historian of Apple, the Apple II and Macintosh. Steve Wozniak and Steve Jobs, as well as *Creative Computing*, *Nibble*, *InCider*, and *A+* magazines were early influences.

Brian designed, edited, and co-produced dozens of books including: *Nibble Viewpoints: Business Insights From The Computing Revolution, Cyber Jack: The Adventures of Robert Clardy and Synergistic Software, Synergistic Software: The Early Games, The Colossal Computer Cartoon Book: Enhanced Edition, All About Applesoft: Enhanced Edition, Graphically Speaking: Enhanced Edition, What's Where in the Apple: Enhanced Edition*, and *The WOZPAK: Special Edition* – an important Apple II historical book with Steve Wozniak's restored original, technical handwritten notes. Brian is also the author of *The Etch-a-Sketch and Other Fun Programs*.

He passionately preserves and archives all facets of Apple's history, and noteworthy companies such as Beagle Bros and Applied Engineering, featured on AppleArchives.com. His writing, interviews and books are featured on the technology news site CallApple.org and in *Call-A.P.P.L.E.* magazine that he co-produces as an A.P.P.L.E. board member. Brian also co-produced the retro iOS game *Structris*.

In 2005, Brian was cast as an extra in Joss Whedon's movie *Serenity*, leading him to being a producer and director for the documentary film *Done The Impossible: The Fans' Tale of Firefly & Serenity*. He brought some of the *Firefly* cast aboard his Browncoat Cruise and recruited several of the *Firefly* cast to appear in a film for charity. Throughout these experiences, he develops close personal relationships with many actors, authors, and computer industry luminaries. Brian speaks about his adventures to large audiences at conventions around the country.

Bill Martens

Bill Martens is a systems engineer specializing in office infrastructures and has been programming since 1976. The DEC PDP 11/40 with ASR-33 Teletypes and CRT's were his first computing platforms with his first forays in the Apple world coming with the Apple II computer.

Influences in Bill's computing life came from *Byte* magazine, *Creative Computing* magazine, and *Call-A.P.P.L.E.* magazine as well as his mentors Samuel Perkins, Don Williams, Joff Morgan, and Mike Christensen.

Bill is the author of *ApPilot/W1*, *Beyond Quest*, *The Anatomy of an EAMON*, and multiple EAMon adventure games, as well as a co-producer of many books including *What's Where in the Apple: Enhanced Edition*, *The WOZPAK: Special Edition*, *Nibble Viewpoints: Business Insights From The Computing Revolution*, and co-programmer for the iOS version of the retro game *Structris*. He has written many articles which have appeared in user group newsletters and magazines such as *Call-A.P.P.L.E.*.

Bill worked for Apple Pugetsound Program Library Exchange (A.P.P.L.E.) under Val Golding and Dick Hubert as a data manager and programmer in the 1980s, and is the current president of the A.P.P.L.E. user group established in 1978. He reorganized A.P.P.L.E. and restarted *Call-A.P.P.L.E.* magazine in 2002. He is the production editor for the A.P.P.L.E. website CallApple.org, writes science fiction novels in his spare time, and is a retired semi-pro football player.

CONTENTS

BLANKENSHIP BASIC

CHAPTER 1
Introduction to BBASIC

Congratulations on your purchase of *Blankenship BASIC*. Our free disk image is available at: www.callapple.org. It is one of the most powerful and easy to use languages for the Apple II line of computers. When the Apple was first introduced in the mid-1970s, there was only one high-level language available – Applesoft. Now, more than a decade later, the choices are so numerous that it can sometimes be confusing. As you begin your quest for the perfect language, you must first decide if you want an interpreter or a compiler.

Interpreters (like Applesoft) are very easy to use because they are interactive. You can make the changes to your program and see the results almost immediately. When an error occurs, and interpreter let you print the value of the variables to help you find the problem. If you grew up on Applesoft, you probably take these things for granted.

A compiler is not nearly as friendly. The programming environment for a compiler typically consists of an editor, a compiler, an assembler, and a linker. You start by creating your source code with the editor and saving it to disk. When the compiler is run, it reads the source file and create an ASM file for the assembler. Once the assembler is loaded, it can translate the ASM file into re-locatable object code. Only when the linker has finished its work will you have a machine language program (that may be twice as large as the equivalent interpreted version) that is ready to run. If an error occurs anytime during the process, this lengthy sequence must be repeated from the beginning.

After reading the above discussion, you might wonder why anyone would choose a compiler over an interpreter. The answer is speed. Even though it takes much longer to develop and debug a program using a compiler, the final code often runs several times faster than an interpreter version. After their first confrontation with a compiler, though, many people decide that the time it takes a program to execute is often far less important than the time it takes to write it.

Design Objectives

After buying my first Apple II computer and programming with Applesoft for a while, I start looking for a programming language that offered the best features of both compilers and interpreters. I wanted to maintain the interactive simplicity of an interpreter. Since Apple II software was simple and widely used, I wanted as much compatibility as possible. I also wanted a modern structured language with named procedures and enough control structures to illuminate the nasty GOTO statement *entirely*.

Finally I wanted a variety of new commands that would (1) make programming easier, and (2) increase the execution speed to the point where an interpreter could be used for many applications that would normally require a compiler.

These objectives seemed very lofty when I first bought my Apple II. By 1980, though, many of my desires were already available as Applesoft ampersand (&) extensions, so I knew my expectations were achievable. Unfortunately in order to satisfy even a subset of my goals, I would have had to purchase numerous packages at $30 or $40 each. Even if I chose to buy them, the packages would require most of the available memory and even if there was enough room for all of them, there would almost certainly be compatibility problems between them.

I finally decided that if I wanted the perfect Apple II language, I was going to have to write it myself. As I began to design the language, it quickly became apparent that it I would have to be more than a program. In order to achieve both power and simplicity, I needed a system capable of integrating many utilities into one compatible, easy to use, package. Because of memory limitations, this new language would have to be coded very efficiently and its capabilities chosen very carefully. In order to further conserve memory, existing ROM routines would have to be used whenever possible.

I decided to start with Applesoft and expand it using the Ampersand (&) vector. The first step was to add modern control structures (similar to those in Pascal) to permit programs to flow more logically. Proper structures not only make life easier for the experienced programmer, they also keep beginners from developing bad habits. Although my control structures made designing programs easier, the "&" cluttered up the listings.

To solve this problem I added an editor that automatically translated each new command into its Ampersand (&) equivalent. A new list command converted the commands for output and format of the listings. Since this process was totally invisible to the user it provided a truly professional-looking way to expand Applesoft.

I was so enthused with my new system that I wanted to add dozens of additional features, but memory limitations soon forced me to pick my extensions carefully. Although BBASIC could not be all things to all people, I am very pleased with the final product. Here is a summary of the features that made it to the present version:

Graphics

1. VTAB, HTAB, HOME, INVERSE, PRINT, etc. work in HI-RES.

2. DRAW, USING provides fast and easy IBM-type shapes.

3. HSCRN determines if HI-RES points are ON or OFF.

4. BOX and BOXFILL for HI-RES.

Editor

1. Autonum and Renum.

2. Insert and Delete.

3. List and edit procedures by name.

Compatibility

1. Existing Applesoft programs LOAD and RUN normally. HGR2 is the only command not supported.

2. Variable storage is identical to Applesoft. (all local variables)

3. The DOS 3.3 version works with David DOS, Diversi-DOS, etc.

Convenience

1. PRINT.USING makes formatting easy.

2. RANDOMIZE provides a random seed.

3. INKEY and INLINE provide INPUT alternatives.

4. SOUND and BELL aid your audio.

5. And all this in one integrated package. Quit trying to get one firm's editor to work with another's sort or another's...

Performance

1. Built-in commands like SORT, SWAP, SEARCH, and INSTR$ make programs fast and programming easy.

2. Procedure addresses are compiled to decrease overhead.

3. CHAIN programs of unlimited size.

4. Improved garbage collection.

Structure

1. DEFINE and PERFORM named procedures.

2. REPEAT-UNTIL and WHILE-ENDWHILE loops.

3. Multi-line IF-THEN-ELSE-ENDIF and WHEN.

4. Listings are indented automatically.

5. Procedures may be FILED and MERGED.

All of the above features fit into 8K of memory. That may not impressed you until you discover that your favorite editor or sort utility requires 5K by itself. BBASIC doesn't use just any area of memory, though. Most of it resides below the HI-RES screen in an area normally in accessible to Applesoft (when your program is moved above the screen). This means you only have to give up to 2K of memory to get 8K of new code. And since BBASIC uses all of Applesoft as a subroutine, you now have an 18K BASIC for your Apple II.

Structured Programming

Modular design and modern control structures are very important programming and elevations. They make programs easier to design, debug, and maintain because they allow us to communicate with the computer using the same terms we use for logical thinking. Poorly-structured systems force programmers to adjust their thinking to match the limited capabilities of the language.

The chapters that follow will examine each of the capabilities of BBASIC. Since BBASIC is a highly-structured language and because structured programming requires a different philosophy, there will be numerous examples to aid you in your understanding. This book is not, however designed to teach you how to program. It assumes that you are reasonably proficient with Applesoft. (All of the new BBASIC commands are discussed, but none of the original Applesoft commands are explain.)

Answers to Your Questions

If you find you need more help (either because you're not a programmer or because you find structured programming frightfully unconventional), then you may want to purchase *Structured Programming with BBASIC* as described in Chapter 11. It is available separately so that purchasers of BBASIC have to buy only what they need. I am very dedicated to making BBASIC available at the lowest possible price. As a teacher, I am especially interested in providing a low-cost solution for schools that want to use a modern language without sacrificing their investment and hardware.

This book, like BBASIC, is very compact. Don't let the small size for you, though. If you take the time to read the entire book, I think you will find that it contains the answers to most of your questions. Actually, the small size is a reflection of how easy BBASIC is to use. Much of this book is a result of your questions as it contains the information provided by the first six BBASIC newsletters. Now that you have been introduced to BBASIC, let's move along and discover why BBASIC makes programming fun again.

CHAPTER 2

Tutorial

Even though I suggest that you read the entire book before use BBASIC extensively, I know that most people will want to get started as quickly as possible. To that end, this chapter provides a summary of the information that you are most likely to need. Even if you are in experienced programmer, I encourage you not to skip this chapter. It sets the stage for things to come.

The first thing you should do is make a backup copy of your BBASIC Master Diskette. The exact procedure will be different depending on whether you use DOS 3.3 or ProDOS, so consult your DOS manual. Both of these versions of BBASIC look alike to the user, but there are significant differences inside the two programs.

The BBASIC Startup Menu

When you boot your BBASIC master diskette, a menu will appear. The first two choices in the menu allow you to select one of the two versions of BBASIC that are on your diskette. The HIRES Graphics version allows you to use HGR and other HIRES graphics commands. When your application does not use any HIRES graphics, you may want to choose selection 2. The non-graphics version is smaller (mostly because you don't need the HIRES screen), so you will have nearly 10K of additional memory for your program.

Another option in the main menu is DOCUMENTION. It only provides a small portion of the information found in this book. Actually, this documentation could be more accurately described as an advertisement. I believe in BBASIC and feel that anyone that tries BBASIC will recognize its value. I believe you should get to try software before you shell out your hard-earned money. Please confirm my trust by encouraging your friends to purchase their own copy if they decide to use BBASIC.

7

Another menu item let you transfer BBASIC to a previous initialized diskette. This is a very easy way to let your friends try BBASIC. This option only transfers the BBASIC system itself. It does not copy any of the demonstration programs. The DOS 3.3 version of BBASIC has an additional selection that will initialize a new diskette for you (and transfers BBASIC). If you have ProDOS BBASIC, you may run the program "PRODOS.DOCUMENT." It lists a few minor places were ProDOS BBASIC differs from the DOS 3.3 version.

Jump Right in

Boot your BBASIC disk and choose option one from the menu to get into the graphics version. When the flashing cursor appears, type in the following line but do not press RETURN:

```
This is a test
```

Use the left and right arrow keys to move the cursor along the line. If you type a character, it will be inserted at the cursor position with the rest of the line shifting to the right. If you wish to delete the character to the left of the cursor, you can use Control-P (hold down the control key and press "P") or Control-Z. If you have a IIe, IIc, or IIGS, you may use the DELETE key. When you get the line the way you want it, press RETURN to send it to BBASIC. You do not have to have the cursor at the end of the line. The entire line will be sent, no matter where the cursor is. Of course, if you press RETURN now, BBASIC will respond with a SYNTAX ERROR since our example line is not a valid BBASIC statement. If you wish to abort the line, press the escape key. There are many more editing features discussed in Chapter 3, but this will be enough to get you started.

Type CATALOG (or CAT for ProDOS) and return to see a list of programs on your diskette. If you press Control-F for FILES, the BBASIC editor will type CATALOG for you. When the catalog appears, notice that one of the programs is named NESTING EXAMPLE. The name will be NESTING EXAMPLE on the ProDOS disk since ProDOS does not allow spaces in a program name. Load the program by typing in the following line:

Take a look at the program by typing LIST. If you press Control-L, BBASIC will type LIST for you. You may start and stop the listing from scrolling by using almost any key. I recommend the Space Bar. When you have the listing in a pause state, you can abort by pressing either the ESC key or the RETURN key.

Hardcopy Listings

If you would like a printout of this program (and you have a normal printer interface in Slot 1), type LLIST and press RETURN. You should not issue a PR#1. When you use LLIST, BBASIC will automatically turn on the printer, LIST the program, and turn the printer off.

If you examine the listing you will see that most of the commands look like normal Applesoft commands. In fact, you may use every Applesoft command except for HGR2. A few of these old commands have been enhanced and act a little differently. The new LIST command, for example, automatically formats the program. Loops and WHEN (multiline IF-THEN-ELSE) statements are indented to show their actions more clearly. Defined modules begin with DEFINE, end with FINISH, and are called with PERFORM.

You can also use the LIST command to begin listing the program at a specific module. Type in the following line:

```
LIST "HORIZ.BAT"
```

When you press RETURN, the program will list starting with line 1500, which is the first line of the module "HORIZ.BAT". The list will not stop until the end of the program. Use the Space Bar and ESC to control the listing as you see fit.

Run the Program

You run BBASIC programs just like you do with Applesoft. Type RUN now to run the program previously loaded into memory.

You should see a short message telling you that the program will draw four types of electronic components on your screen. It will also ask you how many total components you want. Answer "25" and press RETURN. You will see 25 components drawn on the Hi-Res screen. At the bottom of the screen will be the question:

DO YOU WANT TO SEE IT AGAIN (Y/N)?

Answer "N" to end the program. This program shows how easily BBASIC handles graphics. Let's try a few immediate mode commands to demonstrate this point. Type HOME to clear the screen and position the cursor at the top of the page. Now type the following line:

A$="RRIJJIIJJIRR"

Although it will appear that you are in the text mode, remember that the program ended with your Apple in the graphics mode and we have not issued a TEXT command. To prove your Apple is still in the graphics mode, type the following command:

HPLOT 0,0 to 50,100

A line will appear on your screen. Now type this statement.

DRAW.USING A$

DRAW.USING is a BBASIC command that draws a shape specified by a string, in this case, A$. Refer to our definition of A$ above. The R indicates movement to the right and I,J,K, and M are used for the diagonals. These movements define A$ to be the symbol for a resistor. (Refer to Chapter 5 for complete details on the DRAW.USING command.)

When the resistor appears on the screen, it starts at the last point plotted, which is the end of the line. The resistor will be very small. Type in the following line:

DRAW.USING "2"+A$+"4"+A$+"8"+A$

Three more resistors will appear. Each starts at the last point plotted and will be twice as large as the previous resistor. The "numbers" in the string control the size of the shape. After a "2" for

10

example, each R will move two dots to the right instead of one. Type in the following line:

```
DRAW.USING "DDD LLL D JMKI"
```

This will draw a line down, left, down a little, and then a diamond. All movements will be of size "8" because the default is the last size used. The size may be from "1" to "9" and spaces are ignored so you may use them to improve the readability of the string.

You may want to experiment with the DRAW.USING command before you continue. Type HOME to clear the screen. (Notice that the BBASIC HOME command works for both the TEXT and the Hi-Res screens.) You may use the HPLOT to determine where the shapes will appear. If you don't plot any points after a HOME, the shapes will start in the center of the screen. Don't feel intimidated if you feel that you need more information about the DRAW.USING command. It has many additional features and they will all be explored later. Remember, the purpose of this chapter is just to get you started.

Control Structures

Now that you know a little about the DRAW.USING statement, let's look at the program again and see how it works. Type LIST. BBASIC will automatically enter the text mode before the listing begins. This is necessary because the text on the graphics screen cannot scroll. Look at the listing or at the hardcopy you made earlier).

The first command in the program is COMPILE. It is always required in any BBASIC program that uses PERFORM statements. PERFORM is very similar to the Applesoft GOSUB statement except that you can PERFORM names procedures instead of GOSUBing to line numbers. Names make your programs much easier to understand. The readability of the program is also improved because BBASIC provides modern control structures. Control structures are used to determine the order that program statements execute. You should already be familiar with the Applesoft control structures FOR-NEXT and IF-GOTO. One advantage of having a full complement of control structures is that the GOTO can be eliminated completely. Two new structures are used in this program.

11

The first of these new structures is a REPEAT-UNTIL loop which starts in line 1010 in the sample program and ends at line 1220. Notice that all the lines in between are indented to make the body of the loop more obvious. Everything in the loop will be repeated until A$="N". Another new structure is the WHEN-THEN-ELSE-ENDWHEN. Look at the example:

```
100   INPUT X
110   WHEN X>100 THEN
120     PRINT "X is very large"
130     PRINT "In fact, it is over 100"
140   ELSE
150     PRINT "X is less than 100"
160   ENDWHEN
```

If X>100 then lines 120 and 130 will be executed and everything between the ELSE and the ENDWHEN will be performed. The indenting makes it easier to follow the logic of this decision making structure. BBASIC will indent the lines properly no matter how you enter them. The only time indenting will not be handled properly is when a control structure is left out. (For example, if you had an UNTIL without a REPEAT.)

In fact, you can often discover where you have forgotten a structure with only a quick look at the listing. If you forget an originating structure (like FOR), then the listing will be moved to the left toward the line numbers. The listing will drift to the right when a terminating structure (like NEXT) is omitted.

BBASIC and the Ampersand

As mentioned in Chapter 1, BBASIC uses the Applesoft ampersand (&) vector to add the new commands. Press RESET (CTRL-RESET on some Apples) and the LIST our example program. You will notice that all the new BBASIC commands have been replaced. COMPILE, for example, has become & STORE. REPEAT is & CONT. BBASIC follows the & with standard Applesoft key words so they can be tokenized to save memory space.

I only mention this because I don't want you to have a heart attack if your press RESET and try to list your program. Normally, you will never have to deal with anything but the BBASIC commands themselves. When you type in a BBASIC command, the BBASIC editor will automatically convert it to its appropriate "&" version. When you LIST a program, BBASIC checks for &'s and converts each instruction back to the more readable form.

Although Applesoft ignores spaces when it examines a line, the BBASIC editor is not so forgiving. BBASIC commands will not be recognized (or translated) if the contain imbedded spaces. If you type LIST, for example, the editor will simply pass it on to the Applesoft which will do a normal list.

When you press RESET, the BBASIC editor is disconnected and the Applesoft editor takes control. Don't worry, though, as there are many ways to put the BBASIC editor back in charge. Often, all you have to do is RUN your program. Since the & commands do not require the editor to be functioning in order to execute (only to be entered), they will operate properly. Several commands (such as TEXT) reconnect the editor.

Your first thought might be that TEXT is an Applesoft command, not a BBASIC command. Actually, TEXT was an Applesoft command, but if you press RESET and use Applesoft to LIST line 1250, you will see that TEXT is actually a new BBASIC command. The new command was necessary because BBASIC needs to more between the 80-column, 40-column and HGR modes in a much more complicated manner than Applesoft does. In later chapters, you will see that there are several Applesoft commands that will act differently if they are entered under control of the BBASIC editor.

& I

Another way of returning to BBASIC after a RESET, is to type &I and press RETURN. This command will reconnect the BBASIC editor and leave your program intact. You can tell which editor is in effect by looking at the cursor. BBASIC's editor uses a flashing cursor, even on the graphics screen.

Applesoft Programs

I wish to emphasize that you may LOAD Applesoft programs into BBASIC and they will RUN properly (as long as they do not use HGR2). The only difference you will see is that the BBASIC editor will be in effect for INPUT statements and you can eliminate that by pressing RESET before running your program. You must be very careful, though, if you use the BBASIC editor to alter lines in an Applesoft program. Any BBASIC command (such as HGR) will be converted to its ampersand equivalent and the program will operate differently. (You will have mixed text and graphics instead of the split Applesoft Hi-Res screen with four lines of text at the bottom.)

BBASIC supports GOTO and GOSUB statements only to permit you to run Applesoft programs. These statements should never be used when writing new BBASIC programs.

This chapter has provided only a brief encounter with BBASIC. The purpose was to introduce you to the new environment as quickly as possible. now that you know how to operate BBASIC, you should have no problem digesting the rest of this book.

CHAPTER 3

The Editor

Many first-time users of BBASIC may find the editor a little unusual. If you give it a chance, though, I think you will discover that the things that seem the most peculiar at first will soon become some of your favorite features. The reason is that BBASIC is very different from Applesoft.

A structured environment requires a new way of thinking about programming. As you adapt to this new way of thinking, you will find that the BBASIC editor has been specifically designed to simplify modular programming.

The BBASIC editor is always in effect. You may use it when entering a new line or editing an old one. All of the features are available even during normal INPUT statements. Here is a summary of the primary editing commands:

Cursor Movements

CTRL-B – Moves the cursor to the beginning of the line.

CTRL-E – Moves the cursor to the end of the line.

Left Arrow – Moves the cursor left one character.

Right Arrow – Moves the cursor right one character.

Up Arrow – Moves the cursor left five characters.

CTRL-K – Same as the up arrow for Apple II Plus users.

Down Arrow – Moves the cursor to the right five characters.

CTRL-J – Same as the down arrow for Apple II Plus users.

Deleting Characters

DELETE – Erases the character to the left of the cursor.

CTRL-P – Same as the DELETE key for Apple II Plus users.

CTRL-Z – Same as the DELETE key for left-handed people.

CTRL-W – Deletes the word to the left of the cursor.

When You Are Through

RETURN – Sends entire line to BBASIC (also used to stop a LIST)

CTRL-Q – Sends only portion of line left of cursor (Quit at cursor)

ESC – Aborts present line without making any changes (also used to stop a LIST, stop EDITing, and to abort a long CATALOG)

CTRL-X – Same as the ESC (because Applesoft used it)

Control Characters

CTRL-V – Enters the next character typed, even if it is a control character (verbatim). Control characters are displayed in inverse in the text mode and as special characters in the graphics mode. If you enter the Monitor with a CALL -151, you will have to use CTRL-V to enter a CTRL-C to return to BASIC.

The following characters have a special meaning if they are typed as the first character on the line:

SPACE – Prints a RETURN so that a space will continue a long CATALOG just like it always has with Applesoft.

ESC – Aborts a long CATALOG or a program LIST. If used during INPUT, it ends the program. (ESC aborts most everything.)

CTRL-I – Types a new line number equal to last line number + 1.

CTRL-C – Passes directly through the editor to stop the program.

CTRL-E – Types EDIT for you.

CTRL-L – Types LIST for you.

CTRL-F – Types CATALOG for you (FILES)

Initialization

&I – Reconnects the BBASIC editor after a RESET

EDITIng vs LISTing

One peculiar characteristic about the editor is that it will not list one line for you. If you type LIST 100, for example, the program will begin listing the program at line 100 and continue to the end of the program. As it turns out, you never need to LIST one line in BBASIC. Think about this for a moment. The only reason that you ever listed a single line with Applesoft was to ESC up to it and modify some portion of it. If you wish to modify line 100 with BBASIC, you type EDIT 100 and the line will be presented for you to modify.

I think the easiest way to learn anything on a computer is to try it, so type in the following lines:

```
NEW
100   COMPILE
101   FOR I=1 TO 10
102   PERFORM "HELLO"
103   NEXT I
```

If you are like me, you hate typing line numbers. BBASIC will type the next line number for you is you press CTRL-I as the first character on the line (or TAB on a IIe, IIc, or IIGS). Try it as you type in the following lines:

```
104   END
105   DEFINE "HELLO"
106   PRINT "HI THERE"
107   FINISH
```

17

Type LIST and notice that BBASIC has formatted the program to make it easier to read. As you look at the listing, you are probably wondering why I increment the line numbers by 1. The answer won't be obvious or perhaps even believable until you use BBASIC for a while and accept the fact that line numbers have very littler importance. They are only used for editing. A properly-coded BBASIC program will never use GOSUB or GOTO so line numbers will never appear in the body of the program. This means that a program can be renumbered by changing only the line numbers themselves. Type RENUM and notice how quickly you get the cursor back. Even very large programs will renumber themselves almost instantaneously. List the program again. It should look like this:

```
1000    COMPILE
1010    FOR I=1 TO 10
1020      PERFORM "HELLO"
1030    NEXT I
1040    END

1050    DEFINE "HELLO"
1060      PRINT "HI THERE"
1070    FINISH
```

RENUM always starts with the number 1000 to make sure the left side of the lines will line up correctly. If we started with line number 10, the listing would be out of line at 100 and again at 1000. RENUM also always uses an increment of 10. For structured programs, that usually will be plenty of space for inserting lines (especially with the auto-increment of 1). If you find you need more space, just perform RENUM again.

Your first thoughts might be that you will never be able to keep track of your line numbers if you are constantly renumbering. The nice thing is that with BBASIC, you don't have to keep track of your line numbers. You will see in the later chapters that properly designed programs will be made up of many small DEFINED modules. Let's assume that we want to edit something in the module "HELLO". With Applesoft you would need to know the line numbers so that you could list it on the screen. With BBASIC just type EDIT "HELLO". Do so now and you will see the first line appear for you to edit.

If the line needs editing, you may use any of the commands listed earlier. When you are through (or if no changes are necessary), you may press RETURN (or CTRL-Q) to enter the line. The next line will automatically appear for editing. This will continue until you press ESC (or CTRL-X). You might find this strange at first, but I can almost guarantee that you will grow to love it in a very short time. The real advantage is that you no longer have to use line numbers when you edit your programs. (NOTE: EDIT will also work with a line number. You will usually use this option when an error is reported in a specific line.)

LIST operates in a similar manner. You may LIST 1050 or LIST "HELLO". Both of these commands will start listing at line 1050 and continue until the end of the program. Use the Space Bar to start and stop the LIST, and ESC or RETURN to abort the list (while it is stopped).

Restrictions

The editor is responsible for converting new BBASIC commands into their ampersand (&) equivalent. In order for this conversion to work properly, there can be only one BBASIC command per line. If you enter two BBASIC commands on the same line then only one of them will be converted. (You can still use the colon to separate multiple Applesoft commands.) If you must use a BBASIC command and an Applesoft command on the same line, the BBASIC command must be the first statement on the line or it will not LIST and indent properly. This simply means that you should generally use only single statement lines in BBASIC programs. Actually, it is a good idea anyway because it makes the program easier to read. A special utility is available (see Chapter 11) that can compress your program if you need more space.

Another restriction is that the BBASIC editor will only let you enter 79 characters per line. Actually this is not much of a restriction if you use only one statement per line. The only situation where you might require more characters is a long PRINT statement. When you find it absolutely necessary to use more than 79 characters per line, you can trick BBASIC into letting you enter them. To do so, type in your line by do not leave a space between the line umber and the first character. When you hear the warning beep, indicating that the line is full, press RETURN. Type HOME to clear the screen and then EDIT your line.   You will then be able to enter the same number of characters as you can with Applesoft.

The only problem you will have with this long line is that it cannot be edited at the bottom of the screen (which is why BBASIC tried to keep you from creating long lines). Doing so will cause continuous scrolling. (If this occurs, just press ESC, type HOME, and EDIT the line at the top of the screen.) All editing is done in the buffer and the line is printed over and over in the same spot on the screen. This makes is possible for one simple routine to handle editing for the 40 column, 80 column, and HIRES graphic modes.

Since the editor continually prints to the screen, you must never issue a PR#1 to turn on the printer while in BBASIC immediate mode. Use LLIST when you wish to get a hard copy and always turn the printer on and off inside your program with the DISK command (see Chapter 6).

Sometimes you might need to turn on the printer while in the immediate mode (to print a catalog for example). When you do, just press RESET to return you to the Applesoft editor before typing PR#1. When you are finished, use &I to reconnect the BBASIC editor.

Occasionally, the BBASIC editor might conflict with DOS if a FILE name contains a BBASIC reserved word (such as SORT). If this happens, you can RESET and then perform your command. For example:

```
LOCK SORT.TEST
```

You can then use &I to reconnect the editor. Another way of avoiding this problem (short of not using reserved words in file names), is to use the DISK command in the immediate mode as follow:

```
DISK "LOCK SORT.TEST"
```

CHAPTER 4

Modular and Structured Programming

If you have never used a structured language before, you may have a little trouble adjusting to programming without using GOTO. Structured programming is not just a way to write programs – it is a way of thinking. Old habits die hard, so don't get discouraged if you have problems with this initially. Once your mind makes the "flip" (and it will), you'll wonder how you ever organized a program using unstructured techniques.

Making Decisions

Let's start by recognizing why GOTO commands are used in Applesoft. The first reason is to create an IF-THEN-ELSE decision. The WHEN control structure in BBASIC allows this to be done without a GOTO as shown below:

Applesoft Version

```
10 IF NOT (X>Y) THEN 40
20 PRINT "X IS LARGER"
30 GOTO 50
40 PRINT "Y IS LARGER"
50 REM REST OF PROGRAM
```

BBASIC Version

```
10 WHEN X>Y THEN
20    PRINT "X IS LARGER"
30 ELSE
40    PRINT "Y IS LARGER"
50 ENDWHEN
```

If the decision following the WHEN is true, then all lines between the WHEN and the ELSE will be executed and all the lines between the ELSE and the ENDWHEN will be skipped. If the decision is false, then only the lines between the ELSE and the ENDWHEN will be executed. Not only can you place as many lines as you need between the WHEN and the ELSE (or the ELSE and ENDWHEN), but you can also nest WHEN statements inside of each other. BASIC knows which ELSE and which ENDWHEN goes with each WHEN and will indent the listing so that it is easy for you

21

to read. Every WHEN must have an ENDWHEN, but the ELSE is optional. The example programs below show two ways of making the same decision. See if you can find a simpler way.

Example Program 1

```
100   INPUT X,Y
110   WHEN X>100 AND Y>100 THEN
120     PRINT "BOTH ARE BIG"
130   ELSE
140     WHEN X>100 THEN
150       PRINT "ONLY X IS BIG"
160     ENDWHEN
170     WHEN Y>100 THEN
180       PRINT "ONLY Y IS BIG"
190     ENDWHEN
200   ENDWHEN
```

Example Program 2

```
100   INPUT X,Y
110   WHEN X>100 AND Y>100 THEN
120     PRINT "BOTH ARE BIG"
130   ELSE
140     WHEN X>100 OR Y>100 THEN
150       WHEN X>100 THEN
160         PRINT "ONLY X IS BIG"
170       ELSE
180         PRINT "ONLY Y IS BIG"
190       ENDWHEN
200     ENDWHEN
210   ENDWHEN
```

Loops

The only other reason for using a GOTO in a program is to create a LOOP. If you think about loops, you will see that BBASIC has a loop structure for every application. The standard FOR loop is perfect if you know in advance how many times the loop is to be performed. If you want to loop WHILE something is true or UNTIL something happens then you have several options. The WHILE loop decides at the beginning of the loop and the REPEAT loop decides at the end. Pascal only has WHILE and REPEAT loops, so it maintains a GOTO in order to exit from the middle of a loop.

BBASIC can eliminate the GOTO entirely because it has the LOOP - EXITWHEN - ENDLOOP construct to let you exit anywhere inside the loop. You may even use several EXITWHEN statements if you need them. The examples below show how BBASIC's loop structures can eliminate the GOTO from similar situations in Applesoft.

Applesoft Version

```
10   REM beginning of
20       program body of
30       loop
40   INPUT "AGAIN?";A$
50   IF A$="YES" THEN 10

10   IF NOT(X<Y) THEN 50
20       body of
30       loop
40   GOTO 10
50   REM rest of program

10   REM beginning
20       some of
30       the loop
40   IF X=Y THEN 80
50       more of
60       the loop
70   GOTO 10
80   REM rest of program
```

BBASIC Version

```
10   REPEAT
20       body of
30       loop
40       INPUT "AGAIN?";A$
50   UNTIL A$="NO"

10   WHILE X<Y
20       body of
30       loop
40   ENDWHILE
50   REM rest of program

10   LOOP
20       some of
30       the loop
40   EXITWHEN X=Y
50       more of
60       the loop
70   ENDLOOP
80   REM rest of program
```

PERFORM, DEFINE, FINISH, COMPILE

Instead of GOSUBing to a line number, BBASIC allows you to PERFORM a named procedure. Each procedure must begin with a DEFINE "NAME" statement and end with FINISH. All characters in the name are significant, but longer names do slow down the progress slightly. If the name does not contain any reserved words it does not have to be in quotes, but I recommend them. Use a PERFORM "NAME" to execute the desired procedure (subroutine). The first statement in any BBASIC program that uses PERFORM should be COMPILE. Applesoft penalizes you for using subroutines because Applesoft searches the entire program for the specified line number. COMPILE causes BBASIC to create a table of subroutines and their addresses. This makes PERFORM faster than GOSUB because a small table can be searched instead of an entire program.

You generally should not use IF to decide whether to PERFORM a module or not. The following line, for example, will operate correctly, but it will not list properly:

```
Enter:   2000 IF X=2 THEN PERFORM "SOME MODULE"
List as: 2000 If X=2 THEN & CALL "SOME MODULE"
```

A better way to handle this situation is with WHEN as shown below:

```
2000   WHEN X=2 THEN
2010      PERFORM "SOME MODULE"
2020   ENDWHEN
```

Another option is to use the CASE statement. The following lines functionally identical to the examples above:

```
2000   CASE X=2; "SOME MODULE"
```

CASE

CASE is actually much more powerful than the above example would indicate. It is similar to the Applesoft ON X GOSUB statement. In the following example, module A will be performed if X=1, module

B will be performed if X=2, etc. If X is less then one or more than the number of modules, then no action is taken.

```
2000  CASE X; "A", "B", "C", "D"
```

Modular Programming

Modern control structures are only part of a well designed program. Structures are used to control the flow through a program by deciding which parts are executed and how many times they are repeated.

These "parts" of a program need to be organized into modules. Each module should have one, and only one, well defined function. Poorly structured programs are hard to design and debug because their logic is distributed throughout the program. Modular design lets you concentrate your efforts on one problem at a time.

When you approach a programming problem, break it down into smaller and simpler problems (modules). If these new modules are still complicated, just break this down into even smaller, easier-to-solve modules. Let's look at an example. Suppose we wanted to create a program that would move a ROBOT across the room to a door on the other side. The main program could look like this:

```
1000  REPEAT
1010    PERFORM "LOCATE DOOR"
1020    PERFORM "FACE DOOR"
1030    PERFORM "MOVE FORWARD"
1040  UNTIL FLAG$="AT DOOR"
1050  END
```

The PERFORM statement is very much like Applesoft's GOSUB except that the subroutine can be called by its name instead of a line number. Notice how the use of modules makes the logic of this program easier to understand. Naturally, we must clearly define the function of each of these modules and write the code for this. If a module's function is complex, then we can break it down into smaller modules. Let's look at the "MOVE FORWARD" module for example:

```
1060  DEFINE "MOVE FORWARD"
1070    PERFORM "CHECK FOR OBSTACLE"
1080    WHEN OK=1 THEN
1090      PERFORM "MOVE FORWARD 6 INCHES"
1100    ELSE
1110      PERFORM "GO AROUND OBJECT"
1120    ENDWHEN
1130  FINISH
```

Naturally, we now have to create modules to solve these newly introduced teaks. The new modules may also be complicated so we just keep creating new solutions until the new tasks become simple enough to code without defining new modules.

Since you only have to think about one module at a time, you can concentrate your efforts without being distracted by related problems. After you become accustomed to thinking about programming in this manner, you will find that you will not only more productive but that programming will be more enjoyable.

Building a Library

As you learn to structure your programs, you will find that many of your modules will be general purpose. Since it is undesirable to continually re-invent the wheel, BBASIC provides an easy way for you to maintain a procedure library. For example, you could save the "MOVE FORWARD" module defined earlier with the command:

```
FILE "MOVE FORWARD"
```

File is similar to SAVE except that it only saves the module specified. You may add a filed module to a program in memory with:

```
MERGE "MOVE FORWARD"
```

Merged modules will always be added to the end of the existing program no matter what line numbers they have. After merging, you should RENUM or you may not be able to EDIT some of the lines.

If you create a library of useful routines, please share them with the community. If you wish to contribute please follow these guidelines. Use REM statements in your module to define the function as clearly as possible. Specify what variables are used to pass data to and from your module. If a small demo would be useful then please add one. If your module is called "SCREEN BUILDER" then name the demo something like SCREEN BUILDER DEMO.

To help get you started, let me offer a module for entering data. This procedure could use many enhancements, but it should give you some ideas:

```
1000   COMPILE
1010   HOME
1020   SY= 3
1030   READ N
1040   PRINT "PLEASE ENTER THE FOLLOWING"
1050   FOR I = 1 TO N
1060     READ PROMPT$,SL$,SH$,SS
1070     SY= LEN (PROMPT$) + 2
1070     VTAB SY
1190     PRINT PROMPT$;
1100     PERFORM "INPUT"
1110     SY= SY + 1
1120     A$(I)= SS$
1130   NEXT
1140   PRINT : PRINT
1150   PRINT "THE DATA IS:"
1160   FOR I = 1 TO N
1170     PRINT A$(I)
1180   NEXT
1190   DATA 5
1200   DATA "YOUR NAME (ALL CAPS)--", " A", " Z",15
1210   DATA "YOUR ADDRESS--","0","z",20
1220   DATA "CITY--","A","Z",10
1230   DATA "STATE--","A","Z",2
1240   DATA "ZIP CODE--" ,"0","9",5
1250   END
```

```
1260   DEFINE "INPUT"
1270   REM This procedure will present an inverse field
       for input.
1280   REM The user may specify the size of the field
       (SS),where the field
1290   REM is to be located (SX,SY) and the upper and
       lower limits (SH$,SL$).
1300   REM The input string (including leading end
       trailing spaces) will be in
1310   REM the variable SS$
1320   REM Other variables used are SC$ (the char.
       being input), ST (a temp.
1330   REM variable), SN (the number of characters
       entered so far), and SF (a
1340   REM flag that indicates the RETURN key was
       pressed).

1350   SS$= " ":SF = 0: SN = 0
1360   INVERSE
1370   FOR ST = 1 TO SS
1380     SS$= SS$ + " "
1390   NEXT
1400   REPEAT
1410     VTAB SY: HTAB SX
1420     PRINT SS$;
1430     SC$= ""
1440     REPEAT
1450       INKEY SC$
1460     UNTIL SC$ < > ""
1470     WHEN ASC (SC$) = 13 THEN
1480       SF= 1
1490     ELSE
1500       WHEN ASC (SC$) = 127 OR ASC (SC$) = 8 THEN
1510         SN= SN - 1
1520         IF SN < 0 THEN SN = 0
1530         WHEN SN = 0 THEN
1540           SS$ = ""
1550           FOR ST = 1 TO SS
1560             SS$=SS$ + " "
1570           NEXT
1580         ELSE
```

```
1590          WHEN SN + 1 = SS THEN
1600             SS$ = LEFT$ (SS$,SN) + " "
1610          ELSE
1620             SS$= LEFT$ (SS$,SN) + " " + RIGHT$
                 (SS$ , SS - SN - 1)
1630          ENDWHEN
1640        ENDWHEN
1650      ELSE
1660        WHEN (SC$>=SL$ AND SC$<=SH$ AND SN<SS) OR
            SC$=" " THEN
1670          WHEN SN > 0 THEN
1680            WHEN SN + 1 = SS THEN
1690               SS$= LEFT$ (SS$,SN) + SC$
1700            ELSE
1710               SS$ = LEFT$ (SS$,SN) + SC$ + RIGHT$
                   (SS$,SS - SN - 1)
1720            ENDWHEN
1730          ELSE
1740            SS$= SC$ +  RIGHT$ (SS$,SS - 1)
1750          ENDWHEN
1760          SN= SN + 1
1770        ELSE
1780           BELL
1790        ENDWHEN
1800      ENDWHEN
1810    ENDWHEN
1820  UNTIL SF = 1
1830  NORMAL
1840  HTAB SX: VTAB SY
1850  PRINT SS$
1860  FINISH
```

Giant Letters

Another example of a useful library routine is the
"GL LETTERS" procedure in the GRAPHICS DEMO on your
BBASIC master diskette. It draws large letters for you in different
sizes and colors. If you list the program, you will see that it is
actually more than one routine. An additional set of DEFINE-FINISH

29

statements is used to combine the performable modules so that they can be merged and filed as one.

RESTORE.HERE

Since functional modules are the basic building blocks of a BBASIC program, it is important that each module be able to have its own DATA statements. RESTORE.HERE tells BBASIC to begin looking for data starting with the present line.

Chapter 5

Text, Graphics, and Sound

HGR, HOME

BBASIC has many improvements over Applesoft in the areas of graphics and sound. One of the most advantageous of these improvements is the ability to fix text and HIRES graphics on the same screen (as discussed in Chapter 1). In order to handle fixed text and graphics more equitably, BBASIC reacts differently to some Applesoft commands. HOME, for example, clears the HIRES screen just as it does the TEXT screen. Since I often want my programs to flip to a text HELP screen and back to graphics, BBASIC's HGR does not clear the screen. HGR does however set the color to 3.

When you are in the HGR mode you may use BBASIC's user- defined character set (see Chapter 11 for more details). All of the control characters have been defined as special characters. The GRAPHICS DEMO on your BBASIC master diskette shows these characters. You may use CTRL-V, as described in Chapter 3, to enter control characters into PRINT statements. If you define several characters to be some shape (like a space ship, for example), you will find that the HGR PRINT is often fast enough to handle simple animation.

WIDTH.40, WIDTH.80, TEXT, LIST

BBASIC supports two text screens (40 and 80 columns) on a IIe, IIc, or IIGS. Do not use PR#3 to select the 80 column text as you do with Applesoft. Instead, use the commands WIDTH.40 and WIDTH.80. If you ere in the graphics mode, BBASIC will automatically return to the last used text screen. The BBASIC TEXT command also clears the screen. Whenever you LIST a program, BBASIC will automatically perform a TEXT (and HOME). This is very convenient since the HIRES screen cannot scroll. In order to conserve memory, BBASIC uses Apple's ROM code for handling the 80 column screen. Unfortunately, the ROM code has a few bugs in it reusing BBASIC to occasionally jump from the 80 column mode to 40 columns or for the 80 column screen to clear. This only occurs if you are using the 80 column mode and is usually limited to immediate mode sessions (like entering, listing, or editing a program). Although it is a bit distracting, I have never lost a program because of it. If you get thrown into the 40 column mode just use TEXT or LIST to return you to 80 columns.

VTAB, HTAB, NORMAL, INVERSE, REVERSE

All TAB commands work on the HIRES screen just as they do in TEXT. (You have the same restrictions in 80 columns as you do with Applesoft.) NORMAL and INVERSE also work on both screens. In fact, if you are in the HIRES INVERSE mode, then HOME will clear the screen to all white.

BBASIC has a new screen-control command called REVERSE. REVERSE causes any text that is printed on the HIRES screen to be the opposite of the background. If you print on a white screen, for example, the letters will be in black. White letters will be used if the background is black. If you print a word (or even one letter, for that letter) such that half of it is on a black area and half on a white area, then each letter (or dot) will be of the appropriate color. This is very handy for printing on an "unknown " screen because the text will always be readable. You also won't erase any of the graphics by printing over this.

You should not use FLASH when you are in the HGR mode. It won't damage anything, but you will get usual characters. If you want flashing letters while in the graphics mode, you can select REVERSE and print the same text over and over in the same spot (using VTAB and HTAB).

You can use a dummy loop to control the delay (and thus the speed of the flashing) between prints. The HIRES flashing will also occur if you issue REVERSE in the immediate mode because the BBASIC editor prints the line over and over as described above. If this happens just type NORMAL.

BOX, BOXFILL

BBASIC has commands for drawing boxes on the screen. BOX draws an open box and BOXFILL creates a solid box. Both commands use the last color specified. The syntax looks like this:

```
BOX X,Y,X1,Y1
BOXFILL X,Y,X1,Y1
```

X and Y are the coordinates of the top left hand corner of the box. X1 and Y1 are the coordinates of the lower right hand corner. Naturally, you can use any variable or formula for each argument.

DRAW.USING

The DRAW.USING command provides a very easy way to draw simple shapes. (You may still use Applesoft shape tables if you need to rotate your shapes, but I think you'll like the ease, convenience, and speed of BBASIC's shapes.) As discussed in Chapter 2, DRAW. USING allows you to describe a shape with a string. The characters you may use in the string are listed below.

Movement

U — Move Up
D — Move Down
L — Move Left
R — Move Right
I — Move Diagonally Up and Right
J — Move Diagonally Down and Right
K — Move Diagonally Down and Left
M — Move Diagonally Up and Left

On/Off

N – Turns plotting On (leave trail during moves) DRAW.USING
       always starts in the N mode
F – Turns plotting Off (move without plotting)

Size

   1-9 indicates how many dots to move for each letter. Note:
1-9 must be characters (strings not numbers). Spaces may be used as
desired to improve readability. Use HCOLOR before drawing your
shape to set the color to be used. Let's try an example. Suppose you
wanted to drew a box with a diamond inside it. Look at the example
progress below:

```
1000   HGR
1010   HOME
1020   A$ = "RRRRDDDDLLLLUUUU"
1030   B$ = "F JD N IJKM"
1040   C$ = "F JJR"
1050   SYMBOL$ = A$+B$+C$
1060   HPLOT 1,1
1070   FOR J = 1 TO 9
1080      DRAW.USING STR$(J) + SYMBOL$
1090   NEXT
1100   VTAB 20
```

   The first two lines select the graphics mode and clear the screen.
The string A$ draws the box. BS turns the plotting off and moves to
the point where the diamond is to be positioned. The plotting is turned
back on and the diamond is drawn. C$ turns the plotting off again and
moves to the lower right hand corner of the box so that the next time
a shape is drawn it will begin there. Line 1050 combines the pieces
into one easy-to-use "shape" variable. The HPLOT determines where
the first shape will begin. The FOR loop draws nine shapes. The first
shape will be of size 1, the second of size 2, etc. Notice the variable J
must be converted to a string before it can be used to control the size
of the shape. The final line in the program moves the cursor to line 20
so that it won't interfere with the drawing when the program ends.

BELL and SOUND

You may use the BBASIC command BELL to beep the speaker. BELL is not really any easier than printing a CHR$(7), but it takes a more read able program. If you went a more pleasant tone then BELL provides or if you need interesting sound effects, you can use the SOUND command. SOUND has the following syntax:

SOUND D,F,E

D is the duration and can have value of 0-127. The frequency of the tone is controlled by the second argument which may range from 1 to 191. Changing the frequency will have no effect on the duration. For normal tones, the lest argument (effect) should be 0. You can use E (1 - 255) to create unusual sounds. The best sounds seem to have effects near the extremes (1 or 255). Experiment with SOUND and you will see that you can get lasers, machine guns, etc. The following program will demonstrate some of the possible sounds:

```
1000   FOR J = 1 TO 6
1010     READ E
1020     DATA 0,1,3,10,253,255
1030     FOR F = 1 TO 191 STEP 30
1040         PRINT : PRINT "F =";F;"    E=";E
1050         SOUND 60,F,E
1060         FOR I = 1 TO 200
1070         NEXT I
1080     NEXT F
1090   NEXT J
```

HSCRN

The HSCRN command allows BBASIC programs to determine if a given dot position on the HIRES screen is off or on. The syntax is:

HSCRN X,Y,X

The coordinates of the dot are X,Y. After the command is executed the REAL variable Z will be 1 if the dot is on and 0 if it is off.

Chapter 6

Faster and Easier

In addition to modern control structures end fixed text and graphics, BBASIC has many new commands that either make programming easier, or your programs run faster, or both.

SWAP

Applesoft normally requires you to use three statements and a temporary variable if you want to swap the value of two variables. The SWAP command is not only easier for you, but it is considerably faster. If you need to exchange the value of X and Y use SWAP X,Y. Naturally, you can swap integers or strings just as easily.

DISK

One of the most unsightly things about handling DOS commands in Applesoft is the required use of CHR$(4). BBASIC solves this problem by replacing PRINT CHR$(4); with DISK. For example, you can get a CATALOG from inside your program with:

```
1000 DISK "CATALOG"
```

DISK also allows you to turn the printer on and off inside your program. This is necessary because (as stated in Chapter 2) you should never use PR#1 as an immediate command. The example below shows how to let the user decide if the output should go to the screen or to the printer:

```
2000  INPUT "Screen or Printer (S/P) " ; A$
      :
      :
3000  WHEN A$="P"
3010    DISK "PR#1"
```

```
3020   ENDWHEN
:
print statements in program
:
4000   DISK "PR#0"
```

INKEY, GET

Applesoft programmers are familiar with the GET statement. BBASIC's INKEY is very similar to GET except that INKEY does not stop and wait for an input like GET does. If no key has been pressed, then INKEY does nothing. If a key has been pressed, then INKEY acts exactly like GET. As with GET, INKEY should only be used with a string variable. The following example will print periods on your screen until the B key is pressed:

```
2000   A$ =""
2010   REPEAT
2020      PRINT ".";
2030      INKEY A$
2040   UNTIL A$="B"
```

The BBASIC GET is slightly different from Applesoft's GET. It looks the same to the user except that it no longer works with disk files. Many people have used GET to read a text file that contains quotes and commas. With BBASIC you can accomplish the same thing much faster with INLINE. See the example below.

INLINE

The Applesoft INPUT command does not let you enter much characters as quotes (") or commas (,). INLINE works like INPUT except that it allows any character (except RETURN) to be entered. INLINE should be used only with a string variable. The example below shows how to print a sequential text file that may contain quotes or commas:

```
1000    INPUT "WHAT FILE NAME ";F$
1010    ONERR GOTO 60000
1020    DISK "OPEN ":F$
1030    DISK "READ ";F$
1040    LOOP
1050       INLINE A$
1060       PRINT A$
1070    ENDLOOP
1080    END

60000   HANDLE.ERR
60010   DISK "CLOSE"
60020   PRINT "ALL DATA READ"
60030   END
```

Note: Refer to Chapter 8 for more information about the use of ONERR.

PRINT.USING

BBASIC's PRINT.USING command makes the formatting of numbers very easy. A string or string variable is used as a mask which specifies how the output should look, as shown below:

```
PRINT.USING "$###.00";2.5
```

or you can use the following:

```
X = 2.6
MASK$ = "$###.##"
PRINT.USING MASK$;X
```

The example masks and outputs below show the various capabilities. Assume the number being printed is 23.058.

Mask and Number	Output	Comment
"###.##";123.45	123.45	Use # as place holders
"###.##";23.057	23.06	Notice rounding
"###.##";.057	. 6	Leading 0's are suppressed
"###.00";.057	.06	Keep 0's if you want
"##0.00";.057	0.06	Keep 0's if you want
"$####.00"; 12	$ 12.00	$ at beginning of field
"####$.00"; 12	$12.00	$ floats to front of number
"ANSWER=##.00";6.2	ANSWER= 6.20	Strings may be used
"###.##";12345.67	######	Shows number won't fit

The # symbol is used to indicate where the number should go. When the program is run though, the # signs will be replaced with spaces.

DEL.ARRAY

If you need to erase (not just set the values to zero) an array from memory, you can use the command DEL.ARRAY. This is helpful if you no longer need the array or if you wish to re-dimension it.

RANDOMIZE

The Applesoft RND function can be used to generate random numbers. It produces each number by applying a formula to the last number. The initial number in this sequence is called a seed. Unfortunately, when the Apple II is turned on, it always starts with the same seed. The BBASIC command RANDOMIZE solves this problem by using the time taken to press the last key to generate a random seed. Generally, you should only execute the RANDOMIZE command once in each program.

COLLECT

Applesoft (and thus BBASIC) dynamically allocates the memory used to store strings. This is good because it means that the minimum amount of memory is always used. This process does, however, have its drawbacks. In particular, dynamic allocation requires some memory to be set aside for temporary use. These temporary strings, which are often called garbage, continue to expand into any available memory.

When the memory is full (or if your program needs the memory for its variables), then the string space must be reorganized and the temporary strings thrown away. This reorganization is affectionately called garbage collection. Applesoft uses a very inefficient algorithm for garbage collection, so the process can take many minutes under some circumstances. The BBASIC command COLLECT will collect garbage much quicker than Applesoft.

ProDOS offers its own fast collection process. (Refer to your *Apple DOS Manual*.) Rather than duplicate code, ProDOS BBASIC uses the ProDOS collection process when you use COLLECT. Most of the new code required for ProDOS BBASIC fits in the area originally set aside for COLLECT. This allows both DOS and ProDOS versions of BBASIC to occupy the same amount of memory and to have identical starting points for the major subroutines.

SORT

The BBASIC SORT command is both fast and convenient. You may sort any one or two dimensional array (Integer, String, or Real) by using SORT X where X is the name of the name of the array. All sorts are in ascending order, but it is easy for the programmer to simulate descending order. If you have an array A$ with elements 0-N, for example, you could sort it and print it out in descending order as follows:

```
2000   SORT A$
2010   FOR I = N TO 0 STEP -1
2020   PRINT A$(I)
2030   NEXT I
```

Notice that SORT uses the 0 element, not just 1-N. It is also important to know that BBASIC sorts the entire array. If you have dimensioned an array to 100 and use only 25 of the elements then the remainder of the array (which will contain 0's or null strings) will be sorted right along with the actual data. Generally, this means that your data will end up at the end of the array. This may seem like a

41

large problem, but it is very easy to solve. One of the easiest solutions is to fill the array with something that will appear very large to SORT. The largest number Applesoft can handle is about 1.7E+38 so that works well for numeric arrays. With strings, initialize each element to CHR$(255). If you are having trouble with the SORT command, study:

```
1000    COMPILE
1010    SIZE=100: DIM A(SIZE)
1020    REM   now fill the array with large number
1030    FOR I= 0 TO SIZE
1040    A(I) = 1.7 B+38
1050    NEXT
1060    PERFORM "INPUT ARRAY"
1070    HOME
1080    PRINT "BEFORE SORT":PRINT
1090    PERFORM "PRINT ARRAY"
1100    SORT A
1110    PRINT:PRINT "AFTER SORT" : PRINT
1120    PERFORM "PRINT ARRAY"
1130    END
1140    DEFINE "INPUT ARRAY"
1150    TEXT
1160    PRINT "ENTER NUMBERS TO BE SORTED (RETURN WHEN
        DONE)"
1170    PRINT
1180    N = 0: REM number of names entered so far
1190    LOOP
1200    INPUT X$
1210    EXITWHEN X$=""
1220    A(N)=VAL(X$)
1230    N=N+1
1240    END LOOP
1250    N=N-1
1260    REM   the numbers are in A(0) through A(N)
1270    FINISH
1280    DEFINE "PRINT ARRAY"
1290    FOR I=0 TO N
1300    PRINT A(I)
1310    NEXT
1320    REM   note: NEXT is faster without a variable
1330    FINISH
```

Generally, you will find the BBASIC SORT can be 30 to 60 times faster than comparable Applesoft sorts. Even so, you can obtain even faster speed by using BBASIC's ability to sort two dimensional arrays. When a two dimensional array such as A(X,Y) is used, X is the column number and Y is the row number. The array is sorted by the first column. Each time elements are moved, everything in the entire row is moved. The elements in the row could be name, address, city, state, zip, etc.

This program shows how to use the two dimensional SORT:

```
1000    COMPILE
1010    TEXT
1020    DIM A$(3, 2)
1030    PERFORM "READ.DATA"
1040    PERFORM "PRINT.DATA"
1050    PERFORM "SORT.DATA"
1060    PERFORM "PRINT.DATA"
1070    END

1080    DEFINE "READ.DATA"
1090    RESTORE.HERE
1100    FOR I = 0 TO 2
1110    READ A$(0,I),A$(1,I), A$(2,I),A$(3,I)
1120    NEXT
1130    DATA JOHN,37,160,BROWN
1140    DATA SUSAN,24,115,BLOND
1150    DATA TOM,28,175,BLACK
1160    FINISH

1170    DEFINE "PRINT.DATA"
1180    PRINT "NAME AGE WEIGHT HAIR COLOR"
1190    PRINT "-----------------------------"
1200    FOR I = 0 TO 2
1210    PRINT A$(0,I);
1220    HTAB 8: PRINT A$(1,I);
1230    HTAB 14: PRINT A$(2,I);
1240    HTAB 23 : PRINT A$(3,I);
1250    NEXT
1260    FINISH
```

```
1270   DEFINE "SORT.DATA"
1280   PRINT
1290   PRINT "SORT USING WHICH COLUMN?"
1300   PRINT " 1.   NAME"
1310   PRINT " 2.   AGE"
1320   PRINT " 3.   WEIGHT"
1330   PRINT " 4.   HAIR COLOR"
1340   PRINT
1350   INPUT "INPUT NUMBER or YOUR CHOICE ";C
1360   C = C - 1
1370   PRINT
1380   FOR I = 0 TO 2
1390   SWAP A$(0,1),A$(C,I)
1400   NEXT
1410   SORT A$
1420   FOR I = 0 TO 2
1430   SWAP A$(0,I), A$(C,I)
1440   NEXT
1450   FINISH
```

Sometimes (especially with disk files) it is better never actually to move the data. Instead, a system of pointers can be used to keep track of the desired order. The simple program below shows how pointers can be used to manage six students and the grades they made on four tests:

```
1000   COMPILE
1010   PERFORM "READ.DATA "
1020   TEXT
1030   PRINT "BELOW ARE THE UNSORTED NAMES AND GRADBS"
1040   PRINT
1050   PERFORM "PRINT.  DATA"
1060   SORT NAME$
1070   PRINT
1080   PRINT "USING POINTERS MEANS YOU NEVER MOVE THE
       DATA"
1090   PRINT
1100   PERFORM "PRINT.DATA"
1110   END
```

```
1120    DEFINE "READ.DATA"
1130    RESTORE.HERE
1140    READ NS
1150    DIM NAME$(1,NS-1)
1160    FOR SN = 0 TO NS-1
1170    READ NAME$(0,SN)
1180    NAME$(1,SN) = STR$(SN)
1190    NEXT
1200    READ NT
1210    DIM G(NS-1,NT-1)
1220    FOR TN = 0 TO NT-1
1230    FOR SN = 0 TO NS-1
1240    READ G(SN,TN)
1250    NEXT
1260    NEXT
1270    DATA 6
1280    DATA SMITH,JONES,BLANKENSHIP,MILLS,BLACK,WILLIAMS
1290    DATA 4
1300    DATA 66,75,85,82,91,81
1310    DATA 72,73,89,80,96,78
1320    DATA 53,79,81,90,100,92
1330    DATA 78,71,86,79,94,83
1340    FINISH

1350    DEFINE "PRINT.DATA"
1360    PRINT "NAME ";
1370    FOR I = 1 TO NT
1380    PRINT " TT" I;
1390    NEXT
1400    PRINT: PRINT
1410    FOR SN = 0 TO NS-1
1420    WHEN LEN(NAME$(0,SN)) >= 10THEN
1430    PRINT LEFT$(NAMES(0,SN),10) ;
1440    ELSE
1450    PRINT NAME$(0,SN);
1460    PRINT SPC(10-LEN(NAMES(0,SN)));
1470    ENDWHEN
1480    FOR TN = 0 TO NT-I
1490    PT = VAL (NAME$(1,SN))
1500    PRINT.USING "####";G(PT,TN)
1510    NEXT
```

```
1520   PRINT
1530   NEXT
1540   FINISH

1550   DEFINE "VARIABLE DOCUMENTATION"
1560   REM NS - number of students
1570   REM NT - number of tests
1580   REM SN - student number
1590   REM TN - test number
1600   REM PT - pointer
1610   REM G - array for grades
1620   REM NAME$ - array for names end pointers
1630   FINISH
```

SEARCH

When you need to search an array with Applesoft you have to use a loop, which can be very time consuming. BBASIC provides an extremely fast SEARCH command for searching arrays. SEARCH N,X,B,C means to search for the Nth occurrence or X in the array B (Integer, String, or Real). If no match is found, then the real variable will be set to -1. Otherwise, C is equal to the position in the array that X was found. The module below shows how to list all occurrences of a user specified string in the array A$.

```
2000   DEFINE "PRINT.ALL"
2010   INPUT "SEARCH FOR WHAT " ; X$
2020   N=1
2030   REPEAT
2040   SEARCH N,X$,A$,P
2050   IF P>-1 THEN PRINT "FOUND AT ";P
2060   N = N + 1
2070   UNTIL P= -1
2080   FINISH
```

When searching a string array, the second argument in the SEARCH command just be a string variable (and not a formula or a literal string), This restriction does not apply to numeric arrays.

INSTR$

The INSTR$ command lets you search one string for the occurrence of another. INSTR$ N,X$,B$,C searches for the Nth occurrence of X$ in B$ and sets the real variable C equal to the character position found. C will equal 0 if not found. The program below lists the individual words in a user provided sentence by looking for the spaces:

```
1000    SPACE$ = " "
1010    INPUT "ENTER YOUR SENTENCE ";XS
1020    P1=1
1030    N=1
1040    REPEAT
1050    INSTR$ N,SPACE$,X$,P2
1060    WHEN P2>0THEN
1070    PRINT MID$(X$,P1,P2-P1)
1080    P1 = P2+1
1090    N = N+1
1100    ENDWHEN
1110    UNTIL P2=0
1120    PRINT RIGHT$(X$,LEN(X$) - P1+1)
```

Chapter 7

Power Users

A number of BBASIC owners have written to ask for a BBASIC compiler. I thought about it for a while, but (at least for now) I have decided against it. It's not that a compiler wouldn't be nice, but the speed gained doesn't appear to be worth the effort required. This is especially true with BBASIC (as indicated in Chapter 6).

First of all, I prefer the interactive environment of an interpreter (as discussed in Chapter 1) over a compiler. Second, and perhaps even more important, you don't necessarily need a compiler to create programs with professional speed. This is true because BBASIC can perform many of the most needed functions many times faster than compiled code. BBASIC's SORT, SEARCH, INSTR$, and DRAW.USING are prime examples. These commands perform their operations 30 to 100 times faster than equivalent Applesoft code. Compiled Applesoft only fives you speed increases of 2 to 10 times, with the average closer to 2 than 10. This often means that interpreted BBASIC programs run much faster than programs written with a compiler. Further, the compiled programs generally will take much longer to write and debug and often will require considerably more memory.

Improving Your Hardware

If you really want maximum performance from your system, I have several suggestions for you. First, unless you have a IIGS, you should purchase an accelerator card. I have an Accelerator IIe from Titan Technologies and I am very satisfied with it, although there are several new ones on the market with additional features. I have never found any programs that wouldn't run with it, and they run three times as fast. Many Applesoft compilers don't offer that much speed increase. And a compiler will only speed up your BASIC programs.

An accelerator card will speed up word-processing, graphics, spreadsheets, and almost everything! Study the accelerators on the market and buy one of them. You'll get a 300% increase in power for only a 15% increase in your investment.

The accelerator won't increase your disk speed, though, because DOS commands are automatically slowed down to the normal clock speed (required by DOS). If you are using DOS 3.3 you can speed up disk access by as much as 500% by upgrading to ProDOS or by using one of the fast DOS 3.3's such as DAVID DOS or Diversi-DOS. If you have a hard disk or a 3.5 inch disk, then ProDOS is a logical choice because of its subdirectory environment. Otherwise, I prefer DAVID or Diversi because they not only five you the same speed as ProDOS, but they are capable of moving themselves into the language card, freeing up an additional 10K of memory for BBASIC. An accelerator and a fast DOS will make you think you have a new machine – but why stop there.

If you really want to see your Apple II fly, add a RAM disk to the above configurations. ProDOS users have one built in. Otherwise, you will have to add special hardware, software, or both. You will find the speed to be astonishing. An accelerator and a fast DOS can BLOAD HIRES screens from the RAM disk so fast you can almost perform animation.

Windows

After you have built your super Apple II (accelerator, fast DOS, and RAM disk), you will be able to do things with BASIC that you might never have considered before. For example, you may have seen windows on the Mac and wanted to use this in your programs. You may have thought about spending a couple of weeks writing a machine language module to handle the task. You might have even seen such routines in your favorite magazine, but they probably only handled windows on the text screen. The reason for this is that HIRES windows not only require high speed to move 8K of memory, they also need a place to put it.

Since each window takes 8K, you may run out of memory very quickly if you open several windows at once. When you realize that your program will also have to manage output from PRINT statements to the WINDOWS, etc., you may put the idea aside, assuming it would be too much trouble.

With a super Apple II, you don't have to resort to machine language. I was able to develop a simple BBASIC windowing system in less than an hour. The number of windows open at any time is limited only by your (RAM) disk space. When each window is closed, the previous screen is restored exactly as it was. Even the cursor is returned to its original position. The following program demonstrates my windows. FILE these routines on your library disk and MERGE this into your programs whenever you need windows.

```
1000    COMPILE
1010    HGR
1020    HOME
1030    WNUM= 0
1040    PRINT " Windows Demo" : PRINT
1050    INPUT " HOW MANY WINDOWS TO OPEN ";N
1060    FOR I = 1 TO N
1070    INPUT "WL,WR,WT,WB "; WL,WR,WT,WB
1080    PERFORM "OPEN WINDOW "
1090    PRINT "THIS IS WINDOW NUMBER ";I
1100    INPUT "PRESS RETURN TO CONTINUE";A$
1110    NEXT
1120    FOR I = 1 TO N
1130    INPUT " PRESS RETURN "; A$
1140    PERFORM "CLOSE WINDOW"
1150    NEXT
1160    END

1170    DEFINE "WINDOW ROUTINES"

1180    DEFINE "OPEN WINDOW"
1190    POKE 17362,165 : POKE 17363,34
1200    WNUM= WNUM + 1
1210    REM save vital information
1220    FOR W = 0 TO 5
1230    WSIZE(W,WNUM)= PBBK (32 + W)
1240    NEXT
```

```
1250   DISK "BSAVE WINDOW# "; WNUM; ", A$2000,L$2000"
1260   REM   create new window
1270   HCOLOR= 0
1280   BOXFILL WL * 7,WT * 8,WR * 7,WB * 8
1290   HCOLOR= 3
1300   BOX WL * 7,WT * 8,WR * 7, WB * 8
1310   BOX WL * 7 + 3,WT * 8 + 3,WR * 7 - 3,WB * 8 - 3
1320   WL = WL + 1 : WR = WR - 1
1330   WT = WT + 1 : WB = WB - 1
1340   POKE 32,WL : POKE 33,WR
1350   POKE 34,WT: POKE 35,WB
1360   REM   get into window
1360   VTAB WT + 1 : HTAB WL + 1
1370   FINISH

1380   DEFINE "CLOSE WINDOW "
1390   REM   restore everything as it was
1400   FOR W = 0 TO 5
1410   POKE 32 + W,WSIZE(W, WNUM)
1420   NEXT
1430   DISK " BLOAD WINDOW#" ; WNUM
1440   DISK " DELETE WINDOW# " ; WNUM
1450   WNUM= WNUM - 1
1460   FINISH
1470   FINISH
```

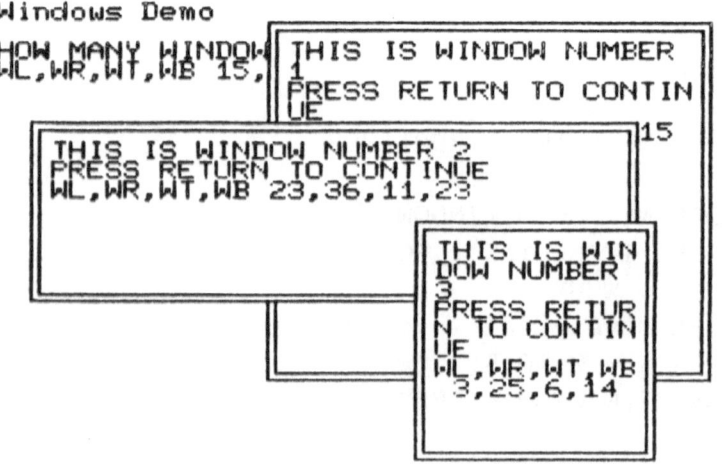

Applesoft uses locations 32-35 (decimal) to hold the size of the window (for scrolling text and wrapping PRINT statements). BBASIC not only supports text windows just like Applesoft, but it also handles HIRES windows with two differences. TEXT windows use location 33 to hold the window width. BBASIC HIRES windows use location 33 to hold the HTAB of the right side of the window. The second difference is that text in a HIRES window cannot scroll.

I also discovered a small error in the internal BBASIC window routines while working on this program. Line 1190 corrects the problem and should be included in any program that uses HIRES windows.

If you run this program on a normal Apple II it will be very slow. On a super Apple II, though, windows open and close almost instantaneously. Any one of the three recommended improvements will help a little. Together, the speed will make your heart flutter. WARNING: If you ever try a super Apple II, you will never be satisfied with anything less.

CHAIN

One of the biggest reasons for having a RAM disk is the BBASIC CHAIN command. The syntax is CHAIN "PROGRAM. NAME" where PROGRAM. NAME is the name of a program that your program wants to run. (Note : CHAIN requires Apple's CHAIN program to be on your disk. It has been licensed from Apple and comes on your BBASIC disk. You can also find it on your DOS 3.3 Master.)

The new program is loaded and executed just as if you had run it with a DISK "RUN PROGRAM. NAME" with one exception: CHAIN maintains all the variables so they can be used by the second program. If you break down your program into appropriate segments, your program can be as large as your available disk space. And with the super Apple's RAM disk, each segment will load with very little decrease in performance. The RAM disk can also be used to hold arrays larger than memory (using random access files). The file variables will be slower than a normal array, but a super Apple II makes their use very acceptable.

Local Variables

Occasionally someone writes to ask why BBASIC does not support local variables. There are really two reasons. First, local variables make interpreters very slow and memory-hungry. Second, and perhaps more important, I wanted to maintain total compatibility with Applesoft's format for storing variables. Doing so lets you use most third party Applesoft enhancements and utilities with BBASIC. Even with this explanation, some people still want to use local variables.

Since I don't have any immediate plans for adding local variables to BBASIC, I thought I would show you how they can be simulated. The basic premise is to create a stack (the array SS) for saving and passing variables. The following demo program shows a simple method for implementing this idea. If two stacks were used (one for passing and one for saving variables), the implementation might be a little easier, but this should get you started (assuming you're interested in exploring local variables).

This program uses the fact that N!=N*(N-1)! to allow factorials to be calculated with a subroutine that calls itself (something that normally cannot be done unless the language supports local variables). This example is only meant to be an educational exercise, but with a little work, you might develop a useful utility.

```
1000   COMPILE
1010   PERFORM "INITIALIZATION"
1020   HOME
1030   PRINT "N","N!"
1040   PRINT " ----------------------"
1050   FOR I = 1 TO 10
1060   SS=SS + 1:SS(SS) = I: REM PUSH NUMBER ON STACK
1070   PERFORM "FACTORIAL"
1080   NF=SS(SS): SS=SS -1:REM PULL ANSWER FROM STACK
1090   PRINT I, NF
1100   NEXT

1110   DEFINE "FACTORIAL"
1120   REM THIS PROCEDURE WILL FIND THE FACTORIAL or
       THE ITEM ON THE STACK AND
```

```
1130   REM PLACE ANSWER BACK ON STACK IN ITS PLACE
1140   REM ALL VARIABLES USED WILL BE SAVED AND
       RESTORED MAKING IT RE-ENTRANT
1150   SS= SS + 1: SS(SS) = N: REM SAVE VARIABLE N
1160   SS= SS + 1:SS(SS) = NF : REM SAVE VARIABLE NF
1170   N= SS(SS - 21 : REM GET NUMBER OFF STACK
1180   WHEN N = 1 THEN
1190   SS(SS - 2) = 1: REM PUSH ANSWER ON STACK
1200   ELSE
1210   N= N - 1
1220   SS= SS + 1
1230   SS(SS) = N
1240   PERFORM "FACTORIAL"
1250   NF= SS(SS):SS = SS - 1: REM GET ANSWER OFF STACK
1260   NF= NF* (N + 1) : REM CALCULATE NEW ANSWER
1270   SS(SS- 2) = NF: REM AND PLACE IT ON THE STACK
1280   ENDWHEN
1290   REM RESTORE VARIABLES USED TO THEIR ORIGINAL VALUE
1300   NF= SS(SS)
1310   SS= SS - 1
1320   N= SS(SS)
1330   SS= SS - 1
1340   FINISH

1350   DEFINE "INITIALIZATION"
1360   DIM SS(100)
1370   SS= 1
1380   REM SS() IS THE STACK
1390   REM SS IS THE STACK POINTER
1400   REM FOR PROGRAMS USING STRINGS, USE S$(S)
1410   FINISH
```

VECTOR

I have tried to include in BBASIC most of the features you normally will need. However, I realize that sometimes you will have an application that requires something I have left out. Often that means that you will have to write your own ampersand extensions. Since BBASIC already uses the ampersand vector, I wanted a simple way for you to interface new extensions. The BBASIC command VECTOR help solve this problem.

For example, let's assume you write a routine that starts at $300 (768 decimal). Let's also assume that you normally call your routine with the command "& A,B,C" and that it determines which is bigger (A or B) and puts the answer in the variable C. In order to use your routine with BBASIC, you must do three things. First, your program must load your routine. Second, you must use VECTOR to tell BBASIC where to go when it finds a non-BBASIC ampersand command.

Finally, you need to use a double ampersand when calling your routine. The double ampersand ensures that Applesoft's "get character" pointer will point to the second ampersand and your program can follow the normal rules for Applesoft ampersand extensions. The lines below show how these three requirements can be set:

```
2000  DISK "BLOAD NAME, A$300"
2010  VECTOR 768
2020  && A,B,C
```

Some extensions will use BBASIC reserved words and may cause you trouble. If you cannot get by without using reserved words, try to solve the problem by PEEKing BBASIC's vector and saving it. POKE in your vector, execute your command, and restore BBASIC's vector. In some cases, you might also need to turn off the BBASIC editor with a DISK "IN#0". You can turn it back on with an &I inside your program.

This technique should allow any ampersand routine to work with BBASIC as long as there are no memory conflicts.

CHAPTER 8

Handling Errors

Applesoft has the ONERR GOTO statement to help your program deal with errors. Rather than duplicate the error-handling code, BBASIC makes as much use of ONERR as possible. The first problem I had to fix was that when an error occurs, ONERR transfers execution to a specified line number. Since BBASIC's RENUM command does not alter any line numbers in the body or the program, the use or RENUM would make ONERR very difficult. Consequently, RENUM will not renumber any line numbers above 59904 (I use 60000). You should place each of your error-handling routines at 60000 or greater.

Applesoft ONERR Bug

As indicated in Apple's documentation, there is a bug in the Applesoft ROM that prevents proper operation of the ONERR statement. BBASIC fixes the problem with the command HANDLE. ERR. You should start each of your error handling routines with this command. HANDLE.ERR also turns off the ONERR flag. This means that any errors that occur inside your routine will generate normal error messages. If you suspect errors in your routine you could use another ONERR statement, though I would generally discourage such complexity especially since it is not necessary. Let's examine some proper methods for handling errors.

You should not expect to handle all possible errors with one routine. In fact, usually your program can test for most errors by using more conventional means. For example, suppose your program asks the user to enter two numbers that are going to be used in a division problem. Instead of using ONERR to catch a division by zero error, your program could simply prevent the user from entering a zero to begin with. The following example shows how.

```
200 REPEAT
210   INPUT "ENTER TWO NUMBERS " ; A,B
220   IF B=0 THEN PRINT "The 2nd number cannot be 0"
230 UNTIL B< >0
240 C= A/B
```

Even though the above example shows the beat way for preventing division by zero errors, let's see how ONERR can be used to accomplish the same thing. Let me emphasize that I would not use this method, but this simple example does provide an effective way to demonstrate ONERR:

```
200   INPUT "ENTER TWO NUMBERS " ; A,B
210   ONERR GOTO 60000
220   C = A/B
230   ERR.OFF
:
:
60000   HANDLE.ERR
60010   PRINT "The 2nd number cannot be 0"
66020   INPUT " ENTER YOUR NUMBER AGAIN ";B
66030   RESUME
```

ERR.OFF

There are several items in this example that need discussion. First, notice the new command ERR.OFF: It cancels the last ONERR command and should always be used immediately after the line that might cause the error. Proper bracketing or your program with ONERR-ERR.OFF statements can simplify error-handling because you can design different handlers for each section or your program.

RESUME returns control to the line that caused the error (line 220 in this case). Sometimes it is desirable to transfer control to some line other than the offending one. Although Applesoft does not support much a transfer, you can do so with BBASIC. Make sure the potential error will occur in a loop. Instead of using RESUME in your error handler, use the loop terminator to restart the loop. (The loop being restarted must be active; that is, it must be the inner loop if several loops are nested.) The examples below demonstrates this principle.

```
100   PRINT "ENTER NUMBERS TO BE DIVIDED"
110   PRINT "ENTER TWO ZEROS WHEN DONE"
120   ONERR GOTO 60000
130   LOOP
140   INPUT "ENTER TWO NUMBERS ";A,B
150   EXITWHEN A=0 AND B=0
160   PRINT "THE ANSWER IS ";A/B
170   ENDLOOP
180   END
  :
  :
60000   HANDLE.ERR
60010   PRINT "THE SECOND NUMBER CANNOT BE 0"
60020   ENDLOOP
```

The ENDLOOP in the error-handling routine will not indent properly because of the absence of a corresponding LOOP, but it will execute properly by returning control to line 130. The proper use of error-handling routines can make your programs more user friendly. Use this carefully, though. Improperly thought out routines can lock up your program in an endless loop.

Error Messages

In addition to the error messages of Applesoft, there are 3 new messages for BBASIC. They are:

Unexpected Terminator (error # 17)
A command such as ENDWHILE or ENDWHEN was found without an appropriate beginning command (such as WHILE or WHEN).

Terminator Missing (error # 18)
A terminating command was expected but not found.

Undefined Procedure (error # 19)

The COMPILE command was missing or thename in the PERFORM command does not match exactly a defined module.

(ProDOS BBASIC uses error codes 22,23, and 24.)

CHAPTER 9
Technical Specifications

You may not need any of this information to use BBASIC. For those of you who desire to go where no one has gone before, I hope you will find it helpful.

Ampersand Useage

Each BBASIC command is really an invisible ampersand (&) command. The following is a list of the commands actually used for each deferred BBASIC statement.

REPEAT	&CONT
UNTIL	&TO
WHILE	&FOR
ENDWHILE	&RESUME
ENDWHEN	&STOP
ELSE	&OR
EXITWHEN	&NOTRACE
PERFORM	&CALL
DEFINE	&DEF
FINISH	&END
COMPILE	&STORE
CASE	&ON
VECTOR	&USR
PRINT.USING	&PRINT
HSCRN	&SQR
WIDTH.40	&4
WIDTH.80	&8
GET	&AT
INKEY	&GET
DISK	&POP
DRAW.USING	&DRAW
TEXT	&SGN
HGR	&FN

HOME	&ASC
INVERSE	&NORMAL
REVERSE	&RECALL
NORMAL	&CLEAR
BELL	&ABS
SOUND	&PEEK
COLLECT	&RETURN
INLINE	&TRACE
SORT	&AND
SWAP	&ATN
SEARCH	&ONERR
INSTR$	&GOSUB
BOXFILL	&XDRAW
BOX	&GR
RANDOMIZE	&RESTORE
CHAIN	&HGR2
ENDLOOP	&RIGHT$
LOOP	&COS
WHEN	&IF
DEL.ARRAY	&DEL
HANDLE.ERR	&WAIT
ERR.OFF	&STEP
RESTORE.HERE	&SPEED=

Memory Usage

The memory map for BBASIC is nearly identical to that of normal Applesoft except that the starting point of the application program has been moved up in memory. BBASIC (2.7) resides from $800 to $4C45 ($2520 for maximum memory). I chose to put BBASIC below the program area for two reasons.

First, the easiest (and most often used) place for you to put ampersand extensions is below DOS at HIMEM, so I did not want to use that space. Second, normal Applesoft programs using HIRES graphics have only 6K of workspace unless the application program is moved above the HIRES screen. When this is done, the 6K below the screen is wasted because it cannot be used for program or variable storage. Most of BBASIC fits into this 6K space. Only 2K of BBASIC takes up memory that could normally be used (the area immediately following the HIRES screen). This means you effectively get 8K of new code but you only have to give up 2K to get it.

You may use Page 3 just as you did with Applesoft. (I do use Page 3 temporarily for some of the optimizing utilities.) BBASIC does use some additional zero page locations. They are 0, 1, 2, 3, 4, 5 , 6, 7, 8, 19, 1A, 1E, EB, EC, ED, FA, FB, FC, FD, FE, and FF. I should also point out that BBASIC uses all of the Applesoft ROM routines, so you really have an 18K BASIC. After summing up all of the zero page locations used by Applesoft, the Monitor, DOS, and BBASIC, there are very few left over for your use. Generally, unless you specifically know you will not cause a conflict, you should only use locations 9, 1B, 1C, CE, CF, D6, D7, E3, EE, EF, and F9.

The new locations chosen for BBASIC are not used by most programs. The only known exception at this time is an early printer interface card that used locations 0 and 1. The LLIST command falls with this card.

Custom Modifications

Occasionally, I hear from someone who dislikes my editor. Since editors are one of the most personal aspects of computing, I want to help you customize BBASIC to satisfy your requirements. At location $C46 (version 2.7), there is a JSR instruction to $1910 which is the address of the subroutine that accepts a line for BBASIC. You might want to alter my editor or just change the JSR to some other routine entirely.

For example, if you use $FD1B, then BBASIC will use the old Apple ESC-IJKM editor. If you know how to determine the entry point of your favorite editor (like GPLE, for example), you should be able to use it with BBASIC. The only problems I expect you to have are with MERGE and FILE. The first eight instructions in my editor check to see if a FILE or MERGE is in effect and a jump is made to adjust the appropriate pointers. I suspect that you may went to place a JMP to your editor at $1924 instead of modifying the JSR, but a lot may depend on the editor you are trying to install.

For those of you who really want to get into BBASIC, let me provide you with a starting point. The BBASIC (2.7) dispatch table alerts at $FB8. Each entry in the table contains three bytes. The first byte is the token for the reserved word used by BBASIC as described earlier. The next two bytes contain the address (less one) of the routine that handles that command. The first three bytes in the table are B3 71 11. B3 is the token for STOP which is used by BBASIC for ENDWHEN. The address of the routine that handles ENDWHEN is $1171+1 or $1172. Remember, if you don't understand any of this, just ignore it and be happy you aren't a die-hard computer freak. Luckily, BBASIC has nearly every feature you will ever need, so customizing is usually unnecessary.

80 Columns

A few people with YIDIX or other 80 column boards have asked about special support for the Apple II Plus. Since I do not have any Apple II Plus 80 column boards, I have not tried any of the following suggestions. I did however design the video interface for BBASIC in much a way that it would be easy to handle both 40 and 80 columns on the IIe as well as text on the HIRES screen. The secret is that I do not edit the screen memory (which is different in all three cases). Instead, I edit in the Page 2 buffer and continually reprint the buffer to the screen. This means (at least theoretically) that any 80 column card should be easily interfaced with BBASIC.

I'll try to explain the requirements and if you're familiar with your 80 column card's requirements, you can work on a patch. BBASIC already assumes that you turn on your card with a PR#3, which should work for all cards. Turning the card off is another matter, though. Many cards will not fully disconnect with a PR#0. Instead, they require a special control code to be sent to this with a print statement. This is accomplished in BBASIC at address $48C7 which holds a LDA immediate instruction to pick up the code to turn off the card (which is $15 for the IIe).

The only other problem I anticipate is that different cards use different locations for horizontal and vertical tabs. Most cards (I have been told) use location $25 for the vertical tab just like the 40 column screen. This number is acquired by the LDA instruction at $1959.

Horizontal tabs are often different from $24, which is used by the 40 column screen. The IIe uses $57B to hold its horizontal tab in the 80 column mode. The code from $1939 through $1949 determines if BBASIC is using 40 or 80 columns and loads the X-register with either location $24 or location $57B, whichever is appropriate. Later, at $1B73, there are four instructions that reset the locations to the proper horizontal position.

I believe that these are the only places that might cause conflict with other 80 column cards. All addresses above are for the GRAPHICS version of BBASIC (both 3.3 and ProDOS 2.7).

Patching ProDOS BBASIC

Always BLOAD a fresh copy of ProDOS BBASIC before you modify it and BSAVE it before you run it. This is necessary because ProDOS BBASIC has a few bytes of self-modifying code, and saving the code after execution will cause your computer to hang on the next run.

CHAPTER 10

Summary of Commands

This summary of BBASIC commands can serve as a quick reference. For more details, refer to the earlier chapters. In addition to these commands, you can use any Applesoft command except for HGR2.

Modular Construction

DEFINE   Used to define the beginning of a module (subroutine).
Syntax: `DEFINE "NAME"`
Quotes are only required if the name contains a reserved word, but are always recommended.
NAMES may not contain commas or colons.

FINISH   Used to mark the end of a module.
Only one FINISH is allowed per module.

PERFORM   Causes the execution of a module.
Syntax: `PERFORM "NAME"`

COMPILE   Must occur in the program before the first PERFORM.
Causes a table of addresses of modules to be created.
If left out of a program, then PERFORM may cause strange errors.

Control Structures

Because of the many loop structures of BBASIC, any program can be written without GOTO's. GOTO will execute properly so that Applesoft programs will run under BBASIC, but the use of GOTO has been discouraged by having RENUM not support it.

WHILE - ENDWHILE (check at beginning of loop)

Used to create a WHILE loop.

Syntax:
```
WHILE A$=8$+CS
        body of
        loop
    ENDWHILE
```

REPEAT - UNTIL (check at end of loop)

Used to create a UNTIL loop.

Syntax:
```
REPEAT
        body of
        loop
    UNTIL A=B
```

LOOP - ENDLOOP - EXITWHEN

Used to create an infinite loop or one that can be exited at any point. EXITWHEN is optional and any number of EXITWHENs may be used if needed.

Syntax:
```
LOOP
        body of
    EXITWHEN A$="DONE"
        loop
    ENDLOOP
```

WHEN - ELSE - ENDWHEN

Expanded version of the IF statement.

Syntax:
```
WHEN A+B THEN
        do this if
        true
    ELSE
        and this if
        false
    ENDWHEN
```

NOTE: Applesoft's IF is still valid. IF should not be used however, with the PERFORM statement. Use WHEN without ELSE as shown:

```
WHEN A=B THEN
      PERFORM "NAME"
ENDWHEN
```

CASE

Allows modules to be PERFORMed based on the value of a variable (similar to Applesoft's ON A GOSUB).

Syntax: `CASE A; "NAME1", "NAME2",..... etc.`

All control structures may be nested in any combinations. Actual depth allowed is determined by the stack.

Hi-Res Graphic Extensions

HGR - TEXT

Similar but not identical to Applesoft HGR and TEXT.

HGR allows graphics and text but no scrolling.
HGR sets color to 3 and does not clear screen.

TEXT automatically performs a HOME. Full use of all PRINT and TAB commands are supported in HGR. (HGR2 is not supported.)

NORMAL - INVERSE - HOME - REVERSE

Provide the NORMAL, INVERSE, and HOME functions in both TEXT and HGR modes.

REVERSE prints in the reverse color of the background (HGR mode), but should not be used in the immediate mode. FLASH will produce strange characters if used in the HGR mode.

DRAW.USING

Draws based on a string variable that contains any of the following characters.

U – Move Up
D – Move Down
L – Move Left
R – Move Right
I – Move Up and Right
J – Move Down and Right
K – Move Down and Left
M – Move Up and Left
N – ON, Plot with Moves (default)
F – OFF, don't Plot, just Move
1-9 – Cause all future plots to be done from one to nine times. System remains in this mode until a new number is found.
SPACE – May be used to improve readability.

NOTE: Draw starts from the last HPLOT or the last DRAW. USING and uses the last color plotted. After a HOME, DRAW.USING starts in the center of the screen. Every DRAW.USING starts in the ON mode automatically.

Syntax: `A$="6URDL F9R3D NIJKM"`
`DRAW.USING A$`
`REM draws a square and a diamond 3`
`dots apart. The square will have 6`
`dots per side and the diamond will`
`have 3.`

BOX - BOXFILL

Creates the outline of, or a solid box of the last color used. Specify the coordinates of the upper left hand and lower right hand corners of box.

Syntax: `BOX 20,25,100,150`
`BOXFILL X,Y,W,2*Z`

Other General Commands

GET
Appears exactly like Applesoft's GET, but works with my line editor. Also works with 80 columns, but cursor will always appear on an even column regardless of real position.

INKEY
If a key is pressed it performs a GET, otherwise execution continues without action.
Syntax: `INKEY A$`

INLINE
Just like INPUT except that commas and quotes are allowed in the input data. (You may not specify a prompt as with INPUT.)
Syntax: `INLINE A$`

HSCRN
Reads on/off statue of a HIRES coordinate.
Syntax: `HSCRN X,Y,Z`
(Z=1 if point X,Y is ON, Z must be REAL)

MERGE
Adds a program on disk to the program in memory. Line numbers are not altered, use RENUM before editing. (a space must occur between MERGE and "NAME").
Syntax: `MERGE "NAME"`

FILE
Saves a named subroutine from the program in memory to the disk. As with MERGE, a space must separate FILE and "NAME".
Syntax: `FILE "NAME"`

RENUM
Renumbers program starting at 1000 by 10's
Syntax: `RENUM`

LIST　　　　　　Lists the program starting from a line number, a module NAME, or the beginning of program. (If you need to list one line use EDIT.) ESC or RETURN stops listing, any other key will pause. Listings are automatically indented based on first command on a line (if you use a FOR-NEXT on the same line, start it with a colon). All BBASIC commands must be first on the line to list properly (a special packing program is under development). LIST will turn off any slot before printing is actually started. If you reset before a list you will see the & commands.

Syntax: `LIST or LIST 100 or LIST "NAME"`
Any key will pause, RETURN or ESC to ABORT.

LLIST　　　　　　Same as LIST but sends output to Slot 1.

INSTR$　　　　　　Finds the Nth occurrence of XS in YS and places position found in the REAL variable C. C will = 0 if no match is found.

Syntax: `INSTR$ N,X$,Y$,C`

COLLECT　　　　　　Forces a fast garbage collection if available memory is less than 1K.

EDIT　　　　　　Presents lines for alteration starting at the point specified by the command. Use ESC or CTRL-X to abort.

Syntax: `EDIT or EDIT 100 or EDIT "NAME"`

RANDOMIZE　　　　Reseeds the random number generator. Generally use RANDOMIZE only once in a program (valid after any input).

DISK	Allows DOS commands without CRR$(4). (you'll be surprised at how much you will like this command after you used it.)

Syntax: DISK "OPEN NAME"
        DISK "PR#1"

CHAIN	Runs a program from the disk without destroying the values of present variables. Requires Apple's (TM) CHAIN program to be on your diskette. CHAIN can be found on a DOS 3.3 master diskette.

Syntax: CHAIN "NAME"

SWAP	Swaps values in any two variables of same type.

Syntax: SWAP A,B

VECTOR	Sets up address to Jump to other & programs. Jump will occur if command name is different than those of BBASIC.

Syntax: VECTOR 8192

BELL	Produces the Apple bell tone.

SOUND	Produces sounds of Duration D (0 - 127), Frequency F (0-191) and Effect R (0-255). Effect of 0 gives normal tone. Duration gives same length for all frequencies. Effects close to 1 end 255 are the most interesting.

Syntax: SOUND D, F, E

PRINT.USING	Rounds off numbers and prints to desired decimal places. Use I to indicate field length. The mask may be a string variable.

Syntax: PRINT.USING "$##,###.##" ; X

DEL.ARRAY   Deletes an array to free memory or allow it to be re-dimensioned.

Syntax: `DEL.ARRAY B$`

SORT   Sorts a 1 or 2 dimensional array into ascending order. Two dimensional arrays are sorted on the 1st column, and the other columns are ordered with the 1st. First column is the 0 column in the array. (And don't forget the 0 elements).

Syntax: `SORT A$`

RESTORE.HERE   Sets start of DATA read pointer to the present line. Allows each procedure to have its own DATA statements.

SEARCH   Searches the array B for the Nth occurrence of the item X. Position found is placed in the real variable C. For multi dimensional arrays the search is in the order of the dimensions, so use a formula to convert "position" to "row-column". String arrays will match if the item being searched for, matches the left hand side of an array element.

Syntax: `SEARCH N,X,B,C`

WIDTH.40 and WIDTH.80   Select 40 and 80 column modes on Apple IIe and IIc only. HTAB will not work past 40 columns (use POKE 1403,POS as Apple recommends). Once a mode is selected, it will be the default for the TEXT command. HGR text will always be 40 columns.

ERR.OFF   Turns off ONERR GOTO.

HANDLE.ERR   Turns off ONERR and fixes ONERR bug. Should be used to start the module that handles errors.

CHAPTER 11

Other BBASIC Products

BBASIC comes in two formats, DOS 3.3 and ProDOS. Both versions look alike to the user, but there are significant internal differences.

BBASIC Textbook

One of the most popular BBASIC products is a textbook called *Structured Programming with BBASIC*. It is 142 full-sized pages. Although it assumes you know very little about programing, it takes you through such subjects as sorting, searching, disk files, graphics, and even bow to write your own "TINY" interpreter and compiler. It is written in an informal, easy-to-read style with the figures labeled in the text for easy reference. It includes a DOS 3.3 diskette image with all the example programs typed in for you. The book is a replication of a dot matrix printed manual.

Utility Disk

A special utility disk was created as an additional resource. One of the items it contains is a character editor so you can create your own characters for the HIRES BBASIC character set. The figure below shows a screen dump from the editor.

In addition to the editor itself, you also get several new character sets ready to be used in your programs. You get a **BOLD** set, an *ITALICS* set, and an UNDERLINE set. You even get several combination sets such as NORMAL/BOLD and NORMAL/ITALIC. These combination sets are upper case only because the lower case letters have been replaced with the alternate set. They make it very easy to mix typestyles in your BBASIC programs.

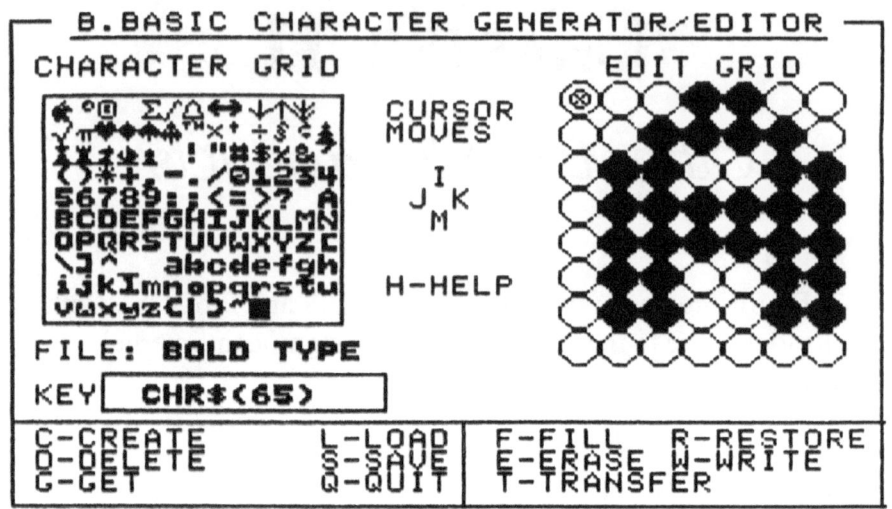

If you have an Apple IIe, IIc, or IIGS, these sets are as easy as typing lowercase letters. Apple II Plus users can access these sets with a POKE 243,32. After the POKE, all HIRES PRINT statements will be in lower case (or bold or italic). Use POKE 243,0 (or TEXT) to return to the normal state. The figure below shows a screen dump of the predefined character sets:

THIS IS THE CGE EXAMPLE. A LIST OF THIS
program will show you how we changed
STYLES OF TYPE. IF YOU USE THE
SUBROUTINE "STYLE" JUST AS WE HAVE IT
YOU SHOULD HAVE NO PROBLEMS IN SWITCHING
SETS. THIS IS NOT NECESSARILY THE
EASIEST WAY OF INTERLACING SETS BUT
IT SHOULD ALWAYS WORK.

The utility disk also contains a set of programs called SHRINK, EXPAND, and SHORTEN. You may be familiar with optimizing programs for Applesoft that shrink programs by combining many statements on one line. These programs won't work with BBASIC because of the special rules about multi-statement lines. The utilities disk has two SHRINK programs that can optimize your BBASIC programs. SHRINK combines lines when possible, but it does not remove remarks from your program.

SHRINK.REM combines lines and removes all REM statements. It is important to have both choices available to you because the diskette also contains an EXPAND program that restores a shrunk program to its original size so it can be edited. All three of these programs are very easy to use. Just BRUN the one you need, and the program in memory will be altered in a couple of seconds. That's all there is to it. You can shrink or expand at any time, without saving or loading or anything. Moat programs shrink to about 80% of their original size and run a little faster. It you always shrink before saving, your disks will seem 20% larger.

The last program on the utilities disk is SHORTEN. It shortens procedure names. As you know, all the characters In a procedure name are significant which encourages you to use long meaningful names. Unfortunately, very long names take up memory and slow execution. SHORTEN is a BBASIC module that can be merged into your program. It converts all procedure names to AA, AB, AC..... BA, BA etc. When a program is both shortened and shrunk, it can be reduced in size as much as 50% (I average about 30% personally). You probably won't want to shorten all your programs, but it you need more space for your variables then it can be invaluable.

Procedure Disk

If you develop general purpose procedures (such as those discussed in Chapter 4), and would like to share this with others, please send them to A.P.P.L.E. via: www.callapple.org/contact. Please use REM statements to document your routine and add an example program if appropriate. When we receive enough routines, we will make a disk image available to the community.

If you have submitted a routine, you will get an advance copy of the disk image. As of the publication of this book, we do not have enough routines.

INDEX

www.ingramcontent.com/pod-product-compliance
Lightning Source LLC
Chambersburg PA
CBHW022114170526
45157CB00004B/1640